ACKNOWLEDGEMENTS

Our heartfelt thanks go to Todd M. LeMieux for graphic design,
Adam Hoyle for computer assistance; Judith Neeld,
Brett Averitt and Nora Nevin for editing.

OFF SEASON

A Celebration of Martha's Vineyard in
Poems, Paintings & Photographs

POEMS BY BROOKS ROBARDS ✍ ART BY NANCY PURNELL

FOREWORD BY RALPH GRAVES

TABLE OF CONTENTS

Polly Hill Arboretum

FOREWORD

BY RALPH GRAVES

As everybody knows by now, summer people who think of the Vineyard in terms of July and August are missing something. More and more of us think that September may be the best month of the year, and if it isn't September, then surely it's October. For many Vineyarders, the Memorial Day weekend is a grand time to open the season, and anybody who misses the Columbus Day weekend doesn't really appreciate the Island. The shoulders of our traditional old summer season have become more and more popular.

But as this heartfelt book of poems, paintings and photographs makes clear, the wonders and beauties and pleasures of the Vineyard do not begin on Memorial Day and end on Columbus Day. *Off Season* celebrates those delightful times when most people aren't here.

Each of us has his own off-season delights. I like making a fire every night. I like being able to take my one-hour walk along Middle Road and be passed by twenty-five cars instead of by one hundred-and-fifty cars. I like all the leaves off the trees, revealing parts of the Island that have been invisible all through the regular season. I don't even mind leaving my car at the bottom of our steep driveway in case overnight ice and snow make it impassable. I like being able to drive through Five Corners without traffic hassle. I like walking through the Island's many conservation properties, which are even more beautiful off-season.

Off season looks and feels and is different.

Three years ago Brooks Robards and Nancy Purnell published *A Magical Place*, their poetical and visual tribute to the Vineyard. Now they bring us *Off Season*, their very personal depiction of their own delights in this Island that is wonderful the whole year around.

Well, almost the whole year around. Brooks Robards has even managed to write a kindly poem about March, a brown, bleak month I would prefer to be somewhere else.

The former Editorial Director of Time, Inc. and Managing Editor of LIFE *Magazine, Ralph Graves is a long-time summer resident of Martha's Vineyard. He is also the author of numerous books, including a mystery set on the Island.*

THE SEASON ENDS

In late August's lush light,
Dark-leafed scrub oaks mute
The wind at day's end. Emptied
Of bird and boat, Great Pond
Laps sand near cattail stands;
Restless clouds edge the horizon
In white, signaling change.

Releasing rain overnight,
Hooded skies withhold warmth
And color from weather-bent brush,
The season's rosehip crop,
Marshy carpets of fleabane.
Swells crash against the sea wall,
Scattering salt spray across the road.

The season's shift does not wait
For seas to calm or winds to abate
Somewhere along the tidal bore,
Dream still mingles with memory.

Gay Head Cliffs

VINEYARD LIGHT

After a summer of few
Come exquisite days
Of clearest light and silence
So pure birdsong peals
From earth's chapel.
Death remains the alien thing,
Waiting in shadows
Still moistened with dew,
The reminder, the presence
That defines perfection.

Cedar Tree Neck

1 1

SUNSHINE RETURNS

A woman patrols the bluffs,
Towed by her dog. In cobalt
Bay waters, a lobster boat
Cuts its line of wake,
Swallowed up in seconds,
And distant as the sky.

The light tells all: its return
Crisps shadows in the foliage,
Limns wind-rocked wires.
Autumn hides in the details,
In birdsong and the peace
That comes with season's change.

Elizabeth Islands

13

CLOSING THE HOUSE

Curtains come down,
Porch chairs move in
With potted impatiens,
Waiting now to wither
 Inside boarded-up rooms.

Softened sunlight
Signals tansy,
Blue-eyed chicory blooms
And honeysuckle vines
To blacken in first frost.

Poison ivy reddens,
And the house sheds summer,
Lets go of what's gone by,
Like trees their leaves,
The heart its heat.

Captain Flander's House

LAKE TASHMOO

All was flat:
Water, sand,
Grass, even gray skies
Over Tashmoo.

All but the dog,
Who was hunting
In the marsh: shellfish,
Bird's eggs, otter pups.

He trotted deliberately
Through salt grass,
Then stopped
Long enough to size us up

Before moving on:
The only other presence
Not swallowed up
By a conjuring flatness.

Lake Tashmoo

AUTUMN IN CHILMARK

Leaves have stolen sun's light
For a last stand by a bridge.
In golden groves of color,
They heat up the woods
Until tree bark glows
Ember black over placid waters.

The fallen scatter their pallette
Over pond's surface in patterns
Echoing summer's world
Or collect along the banks
Against a liquid sky's blue,
Softening the season's edge.

State Road, Chilmark

VANESSA'S WORLD

Fall breezes keep Island air cool
And dampness at bay.
Lavender-berried, a single juniper
Measures the season;
Wind flattens salt meadow grass
Into a beryl berth big enough for a giant.

Silhouetted against water,
Cormorants roost on stone jetties
Marking the shallows of the Sound;
Wild honeysuckle, trumpet vines
And fruited beach plums untangle
Along the road next to Farm Pond,

Where dragons, like rocking horses,
Mark the tidal ebb and flow.

Farm Pond

HARVEST MOON

Full of itself, the moon
Looms large at street's end,
Plays hide-and-seek down the hill
To Five Corners in a night sky.

Along the causeway this same moon
Chases itself across bay waters
Into the stars till it's far,
Far away from mast-lit boats.

Hanging above the harbor,
Moon's light scatters
Into shimmering fish scales
On molasses waters.

Grown big as a wafer again,
Moon moves up the drive
Into a nook between roof
And gable, at home with me.

Oak Bluffs Harbor

LIGHT FIRE

Light low in the sky
Fires leaves of burnt umber.
Shades of persimmon,
Yellow ochre, flame
And russet fan
Summer's embers.

Inside the forest,
A confetti of cast-offs
Layers the ground,
Reverberating
Color off trees
Shadowy and cool.

Hills in the distance
Mute the season,
Soften the glow,
Until lessening light
Sends all sense of life
Into night's chill.

North Road, Menemsha

WORD PLAY

I have squeezed you
Like puppets
In a play world,
Soiled you in my effort
To rouse you.

Now you remain lifeless
Before the power
Of imagination
As it spins
Its frenzied courtship.

Discarded playthings
That you are,
You wait
For me to take you
Dancing once again.

Main Street, Vineyard Haven

HURRICANE WATCH

Sultry, silent air mutes
Even the rhythmic din
Of surf pummeling sand;
This is a time for waiting.

On weather maps
Of the Caribbean,
Tropical storms line up
Like jets at Laguardia.

One woman finds herself
Almost swept out to sea
By a rip and wonders
How quickly her life is spent.

Another loses herself
In memories of the sea
Making itself felt
Wherever she goes.

There light distills
Into rapture, or skies,
Turned overcast, breed
Bleakness beyond despair.

Mink Meadows

THANKSGIVING

On Thanksgiving Day
Sky's pilgrim gray
Took on a blackish cast,
And crimson, fading fast
Over a tangle of trees,
Sent rooftops into dark.

Easier to chart, such changes,
Than those of a troubled heart:
Far from the table's grace,
Fearful, less discrete
Than the stately move of light
Through dusk back into night.

Sengekontacket

3 1

3 2

FIRST FROST

First frost, vanquished
Wherever sun has hit,
Glazes shadowed grass.
Stunned into exquisite,
Crisp inertia,

Leaves stay untouched
By gelid air,
Frozen in time,
Like the body
After its last breath.

West Tisbury

SNOWFALL

When first snowfall
Comes late, you savor
The way it recreates.

Pristine, revisioned
 In floods of white,
Air itself freezes

Into crystal flakes,
Sky a pastel canvas
In the aftermath.

Yes, the world sleeps,
Transformed,
Silenced in its majesty.

Martha's Vineyard Agricultural Society

FRESH SNOW

Hard rain in the woods
Batters crusted snow.
Tree trunks bleed brown
Into winter's white skirts.

Squirrels, rabbits leave prints
Finely detailed as fossils.
Soon a clatter of heavy flakes
Signals snow's return.

Against this new white plane,
Colors spring to life: the stream,
Ice-bound, grows yellow-green;
Old leaves glow a pale brown-gold.

Pines gather the fresh snow,
Flake by flake, on deep green boughs:
Spirit of rain made flesh.

Mytoi

CHRISTMAS TABLECLOTH

A tablecloth loops over drying rack,
Ironing board and upended table,
Yards of linen damp from washing.

Gliding across its snowy fields, the iron
Sends up sweet-smelling curls of steam,
Melts candlewax, darkens nascent stains.

Ready for a family disordered by death
And love's estrangements, it hangs,
Washed clean, pressed smooth, set right.

West Chop Overlook

THE OTHER SIDE

On Lagoon Pond,
As the lifting fog
Sucks sailboats
Out of the water,

You are on my mind;
You are on the other side.

Vineyard Haven Harbor

41

EVERYDAY LIFE

Like pin pricks,
Life's particulars cloy
Into a web of fire
And yellow fog.

Human conspiracies
Laser through me,
Until all surface
Sheen is riven.

I think at last
To smash life's prism,
But you, my cerebral fiend,
Have been there already

With your glass cutter.
So I palm my eyeballs
Gently, like peachstones,
And learn germination
Comes creosote-flavored.

Owen Park

January Thaw

To make this slush underfoot,
Last night's hard rain must have
Turned to sleet unseen.
Neither snow nor rain, its wet remnants
Coat the street with icy mush.

Sun springs out of the overcast,
Freshening yellowed, close-cropped grass
Into the clean, well-groomed look
That comes when sunlight follows
Fast on the heels of firm rain.

Catches of rainwater under shrubs,
A few patches of ice, linger
In house shadows and woods.
Branches radiate a range of browns
Instead of winter light's flat blacks.

Then clouds change back to gray,
Draining vegetation of life itself,
Not just color. Wind-driven
Tree limbs stiffen, bringing
Stillness beneath a blackened motion.

Steamy, roiling fog, dense enough
To penetrate the upper registers of air,
Obscures the last moment's blue,
Then sun takes its turn again,
Prodding gray into the background

And weaving russet bands of light
Among the shadowed, fallen leaves.

Turkeyland Cove

MERELY SEASONAL

Such panic
I keep forgetting,
Is February.
The chill in the gut
Is merely seasonal,
And when the weather
Warms, so will I.

If it doesn't, the soul
Must find its own season.
No absolutes I must
Remember, wondering
Where the world learned
To stand so starkly still.

Cedar Tree Neck

4 7

POST SOLSTICE

In the belly of winter,
Days stay dark, indistinct;
Fog rises from snow
Thickened, crusted with ice—
Pendant, inert in the atmosphere.
While spring stays months away,
It will come, bringing more light.

You must banish despair,
For each hour is another gift.
Each day more light penetrates mists;
Some days it breaks through clouds
With reminders of how soon sun
Will flood the world and bring,
In its brilliance, new life.

Moshup Beach

LEAP YEAR DAY

Last night the seasonal engines
Shifted gears, shot frozen
Sparks as fast as teardrops,
Downshifting back into winter
With icy gusts and frigid skies.

Any seasoned sensibility knows
Balmy days had come too soon,
Brought longings bound to be broken
In brittle air; snow alone
Cures such austere postures.

Aquinnah

WIZARDRY

Mr. Oz, the wizard,
So much friendlier
Than his projected phantom,
Has turned the sky apricot,

Temporarily a flat,
Chalky backdrop
For black spaghetti
Branches hanging
In limp air.

As orange shifts
To pinker hues,
I marvel at the magic.
Once the machinery
Fascinated me;
Now I fashion ways
To dissolve it
Back into fantasy.

Philbin Beach

EGGPLANT FOR BREAKFAST

If you fry it lightly
In peanut oil,
The purple skin
Turns earthy brown
From its egg
And wine batter.

How can you beat it
With a name like that?

Served up royally
By my favorite chef,
I eat this food
Of our gods.

A simple way for you
To say "I love you,"
And me to say,
"I love you, too."

Lambert's Cove

WEATHER CHANGE

My day starts clear with breezes
That pick up strength, grow steady,
Flattening the light in a whitened sky.

High, thin cloud cover
Racks over cauliflowers of cumulus;
Trees rustle, doors creak, shades slap,
Signalling a shift into soothing rain.

Lobsterville

FOR A WOULD-BE LOVER

No alloy of the past—
I did not recognize you
Till our time vanished.

When awareness
Came, I was locked
In those old patterns.

Sadly, I made you
Part of them. You
Found yourself free;

If I had, memories
Would have kept us
Apart, as they do now.

Lobsterville Road

BEFORE THE EQUINOX

Warm winds waft over fields
Still blanketed with snow
Turned soft as old cotton
Sheets. Giddy drafts of cold air
Soar from the snow mix.

With one wave overnight,
The season's magic wand
Turns snow into fog,
Then it vanishes in rain.

Fringes of ice, patches
White-kerneled, remain
From a world once frozen,
Pristinely still without
Benefit of birdsong.

Brine's Pond Preserve

SEASONAL INSOMNIA

I have waited a lifetime
For spring's pale heat
To dissolve the barren soil,
Waited for morning's motion
To let me rise from bed.

I have longed for dreams
To release me from dread
Of night and desire's ache.
The time has gone somewhere;
Where is that hidden place?

Aquinnah

SPRING SOUP

Patches of warm, wet air
Siphon the season's snowfall
Into low-lying clouds.

These mists hang in the fields
As if reluctant to let go
Of the ground and move on.

Not set to loosen its grip,
Cold beckons, insists.
In the woods, horses crash

And lunge through a soup
Of slush, old ice and mud;
The oldest, exhausted,
 Lies down on his rider.

Lagoon Pond

GOLFING OFF SEASON

You describe how to play
The course, each par,
Where to place the tee.

Sunlight on the edge
Of snowbound fairways
Mottles the woods.

I never learned the game,
But off-season it brings me
Onto home ground.

Raised into an icy spine
By seasonal melts, a ski track
Wanders through the rough,

Where cotton candy
Mixes winter's pleasures
With the sweetness of spring.

Mink Meadows Golf Club

MARCH LIGHT

March light does not seduce;
Neither warmth
Nor color clouds it.
Under open skies
It speaks with unrelenting truth
And rectitude of what is dead.

The ground remains raw,
Patched with frost.
No sign of spring
Threatens the clarity
Of this season's measure:
No corner of the world escapes.

The message it carries is plain:
In the end light is all.

Vineyard Haven Yacht Club

A STORM BLOWS THROUGH

Rain, welcome after this dry summer,
Turns Nantucket Sound muddy.
When it stops, you're gone; the house quiets.

It's an old feeling, this clenching
Of the heart. Left behind once again,
I am the parent now, you the charmed child

I can't bear to see go. Brokenhearted,
I ride the wind with you, waiting
For clouds to clear, the sea to still.

East Chop

7 1

BEFORE SPRING RAIN

High-vaulted in a brighter sky,
Gray clouds gather before the rain.

Freeze-dried on their branches, leaves
Turn translucent yellow in the sunlight.

Warmer air mixes with snow-chilled drafts
In a witches' brew before spring rain.

Telegraph Hill

7 3

EARLY IN THE SEASON

Spring snow skids
Into soft drizzle.
Robins clamor,

Bluejays protest;
Wheels of passing cars
Sizzle in benign dampness.

Like cake, streets crumble
From subterranean thaws.
Mildness is all.

Duarte's Pond

YES, IT IS SPRING

Faint green stains
A gray landscape,
Reminding me,
Yes, it is spring.

I feel no joy
At this year's awakening:
Without relish for despair,
I remember too well

The disappointments
Of other seasons,
When faced
With the evidence.

Middletown Nursery

WAITING FOR SUMMER

Wind glazes a surly ocean
With peaks of glair. Up the street
Toward Circuit Avenue,
Battered greenery struggles
To find its way into softening sun.

Water-side, a host of grays
Mutes waves and sand in motion.
Wind wins its fight for bleakness,
Unseasonable but temporary.
All waits for light's return.

Camp Meeting Association